IMAGES
of America

ASSOCIATION
ISLAND

Association Island is within a string of islands on the eastern shore of Lake Ontario separating Henderson Bay from the lake in northern New York State. The islands, rocky shoals, and gravel bars contribute to the exceptional black bass and yellow perch fishing in these waters, the original lure for the incandescent-lamp businessmen who founded Association Island. Artist Emily Anthony created this map from maps that were hand-drawn by early Henderson Harbor fishing guides. (Courtesy of Henderson Harbor Guides Association.)

ON THE COVER: The *Claverack II*, Association Island's passenger ferry, is preparing to leave the island with passengers for Henderson Harbor in 1956. The *Claverack II* was one of several boats used to ferry GE employees to the island in Lake Ontario during its 50 years as the GE corporate retreat and training center. (Courtesy of miSci.)

IMAGES
of America

ASSOCIATION ISLAND

Timothy W. Lake and
the Schenectady Museum

ARCADIA
PUBLISHING

ISBN 978-0-7385-9847-5

Published by Arcadia Publishing
Charleston, South Carolina

Printed in the United States of America

Library of Congress Control Number: 2012950406

For all general information, please contact Arcadia Publishing:
Telephone 843-853-2070
Fax 843-853-0044
E-mail sales@arcadiapublishing.com
For customer service and orders:
Toll-Free 1-888-313-2665

Visit us on the Internet at www.arcadiapublishing.com

This book is dedicated to the memory of my sister, Julie Lake Bettinger, who first introduced me to Association Island in 1972.

CONTENTS

Acknowledgments   6

Introduction   7

1.   Fishing Camps and Lamps   9

2.   GE Takes Over   21

3.   Depression and World War II   33

4.   Glory Days of the 1950s   49

5.   YMCA and Recreation   71

6.   Boats   83

7.   Henderson Harbor   101

ACKNOWLEDGMENTS

The images in this book, unless otherwise noted, are from a personal collection obtained over 40 years, since I first visited Association Island in 1972. Additional photographs were contributed by the Schenectady Museum, recently renamed miSci, and curator Chris Hunter (miSci).

SUNY at Albany professor Gerald Zahavi helped me explain the early photographs of men dressed in costumes through his multimedia essay "The Aural and Visual Dimensions of Corporate Culture Building: General Electric's Association Island, 1906–1956."

Photographs and research materials were also compiled from the National Museum of American History at the Smithsonian Institution, Washington, DC (SI); the Western Reserve Historical Society Library Research Center, Cleveland, Ohio (WRHS); the Dwight P. Church Collection at the Owen D. Young Library, St. Lawrence University, Canton, New York (Church); Jefferson County Historical Society, Watertown, New York (JCHS); US Coast Guard Historian (CGH); North Coast New York Coast Guard Association (NCNYCGA); personal memoir papers of Franklin S. Terry; papers and documents from the Association Island Recreational Corporation, 1972–1973; the Richard and Jill Billings Association Island scrapbook, 1960–1975 (Billings); the Alice "Allie" Austin Association Island Photograph Collection, Maryanne Giangobbe, curator (Austin); *Jefferson County Journal* (JCJ); and the *Watertown Daily Times* (WDT).

Thank-yous are extended to the people who provided photographs, stories, and research material. They include the following: Vicki Catozza, Kay Peterson, Emily Anthony, John Johnson Jr., Karl Fowler, Butch Maitland, Amy Billings, John Billings, Tina Giangobbe Rapp, Lillian Tiller Lattimer, James and Signe McGowan, Grover Moore, Frank Bovee, Julie West, Kathleen Keck, Charlene Keck, Janine Smith, Gail Smith, Harriet and Jeff Averill, Patti Ingram, Joel Wescott, Valerie Shutts DeRuiter, Wanda Hutchinson Primeaux, Harold Hutchinson, Eileen Pretre, James and Mary Parke Manning, John D. Marsellus, Gordon Koscher, Stan Hovey, James Golden, David and Jeri Joor, the late Ann Dulles Joor, John Stevens, Jill Stevens, Eric Ulrichsen, William "Sandy" Conde, Lenka Walldroff, David and Paulyn Eastman, Frances Eastman, Alma Eastman, Eleanor Green, Lamar Bliss, Paul Haggett, Mark McMurray, Ronald and Cordelia "Corky" Peterson, Charlotte Richmond, the late Frank Ross, Dean Witmer, Bill Shull, James C. Bettinger, Ian Coristine, Charlie Millar, Bill Millar, Dan Higgins, Jonathan Fish, David and Penny McCrea, Diane Henchen Gamble, J. Craig Kerr, John Ash Clark, Association Island RV Resort and Marina, and the General Electric Company.

INTRODUCTION

Association Island may have the finest view on the eastern shore of Lake Ontario. With the lake and Canada to its north and west and the calmer waters of Henderson Bay and Harbor to its east and south, it is an ideal setting for watching activity on the water. French soldiers took advantage of its location to build a log fort in the 1750s. At Camp de L'Observation, they could watch for English warships in the lake and for Indians paddling through the bay and harbor. At 64 acres, it was small enough to see all around the lake. Originally named Warner's Island for the Henderson Harbor Warner family, proprietor of Warner's Inn, Association Island is part of a string of four islands connected by gravel bars and rocky shoals on Sixtown Point. Prior to being purchased in 1906 by 10 businessmen from the National Electric Lamp Company (NELC), a consortium of lamp manufacturers, the use of Warner's Island was limited to pasturing cattle, boys' camping groups, hunting, and picnics by fishermen.

Incandescent lamp company owners of the NELC had been gathering at Henderson Harbor and other resorts several times a year to plan competition against their rival, General Electric. Seeking a permanent resort for their encampments, Franklin S. Terry of the Sunbeam Lamp Company, of Chicago, and Burton G. Tremaine of the Fostoria Lamp Company, of Fostoria, Ohio, joined with eight other lamp company owners and purchased Warner's Island for $2,500.

Terry and Tremaine, and the NELC, then purchased 30 other small lamp companies in the midwestern and northeastern United States. However, Terry and Tremaine had quietly convinced GE to purchase a 75-percent stake in the NELC while they maintained full control of the company, keeping this transaction a secret. Soon after they purchased the island, the company name was changed to the National Electric Lamp Association (NELA) to provide a sense of equality among the members. The island was initially referred to as Electrical Island, but the name Association Island was eventually adopted.

In 1910, Terry and Tremaine also convinced GE to fund their million-dollar plan to construct NELA Park, the first suburban corporate industrial park in America, on the edge of Cleveland. Terry and Tremaine's secret would later lead to GE absorbing all of the NELA when the companies were sued for violation of the Sherman Antitrust Act. They settled the suit with a consent decree in 1911, and GE assumed ownership of the NELA and Association Island. Terry and Tremaine made the announcement of GE's takeover at their 1911 summer conference on Association Island. Terry said that various division heads of the company expressed surprise and shock that they had been under the financial control of GE for many years.

With other GE leaders, such as Pres. Gerard Swope, Chairman Owen D. Young, and GE vice presidents Terry and Tremaine, Association Island was further developed. Each summer, GE managers and other employees came to the island from Harrison, New Jersey; Schenectady, Syracuse, Rochester, and Buffalo, New York; Youngstown, Cleveland, and Toledo, Ohio; Chicago, Illinois; St. Louis, Missouri; Pittsburgh and Philadelphia, Pennsylvania; Washington; and New England. Already boasting a two-story, eight-slip boathouse, running water, and electric lights by 1909, the island facilities were expanded by GE with an administration building, dining hall, chapel, town hall, meeting hall and performance stage, elaborate bathhouses, swimming docks, golf course, shooting range, and 160 architecturally unique sleeping cabins. Hundreds of employees were hired from northern New York State over the 50 years that GE owned and operated the island resort.

GE maintained large docks for boats and passengers at Henderson Harbor where it developed a business relationship with Harbor Inn proprietor and postmaster Goodwin M. Snow. Island visitors boarded ferryboats at the former Snow's Hotel dock, kept their cars at Snow's Garage, and sent their mail from his post office. Henderson Harbor hotels, restaurants, marinas, and tradesmen and laborers all provided for the needs GE and the island campers for 50 years. Campers arrived on overnight New York Central Railroad trains at Pierrepont Manor, Adams, or Adams Center, New York, for a bus ride to Henderson Harbor. Upon checking in at the Harbor Inn docks, they would be assigned a 15-minute ride to Association Island on boats such as the *Dauntless*, *Commanche, Starling, Snowshoe, Just Brown, Wahine, Claverack, Islander, Spirit of the Island*, and *Miss St. Lawrence*. Each summer, visitors shared cabins and bathhouses and were given a schedule of meetings and social events for their camp sessions. Food and drinks, entertainment, sports, and social activities were provided by GE.

In the 1920s, a Curtiss "Jenny" mail plane, piloted by Victor A. Rickard, arrived each morning from Schenectady with the mail and newspapers, landing in the middle of the island. Campers organized sophomoric games between departments with elaborate costumes and props. Greased pig chases and apple- and donut-eating competitions were organized for the children, fishing trips were made to nearby Stony Island and Myron Barney's fishing camp, and some visitors took advantage of the island's proximity to Canada and navigated their boats across the border for booze during Prohibition. GE employees also established the world-renowned Elfun Society beneath a large elm tree on the shoreline. GE purchased Carleton Island in the St. Lawrence River, near Clayton, New York, in 1930, with plans to move the resort there. Despite having designed a golf course and demolishing or selling parts of a grand villa on the larger island, the Great Depression and World War II changed the plans and caused GE to eventually liquidate its interest in Carleton Island.

Company expansion, changing times and corporate strategy, repetitive flooding, expensive maintenance obligations, and the satire of island activities described in author Kurt Vonnegut's 1952 novel *Player Piano*, caused GE to pull out of Association Island at the end of summer camp in 1956. The island was donated to the New York State YMCA in September 1959 for $1. The YMCA used it for a summer camp through 1966 and forever changed the island's character by constructing a causeway from nearby Hovey's Island, which was also part of the GE tract. Financial hardship forced the YMCA to put the island up for sale. A massive cottage and marina development was proposed for both Association and Hovey's Islands, as well as a large plot of land on neighboring Snowshoe Point, but it failed to win approval. By the 1970s, Association Island was being used as a nonprofit arts and recreation center and as a training facility for the US Olympic Sailing Team. Fully abandoned in 1977, the island remained vacant until 2002, when it was developed into the Association Island RV Resort and Marina.

Still on the island from the GE era are the first bathhouse, built about 1910; the Black Catte Café; dining hall; hospital; town hall; and employees' dormitory. The boat lagoon is still there, but the boathouse is long gone. Most of the cabins are gone, auctioned off in the 1970s. A few of the original cabins remain scattered around Henderson Harbor. Elfun Square still juts out into the lake, but the Elfun elm tree died from disease and was removed in the early 1970s. A boulder monument dedicated in 1946 with a World War II memorial plaque is still on the island but the plaque is gone. After many years of darkness, electric lights glow again on Association Island. Today, like they did in the 1750s, Association Island campers still have the best view of the eastern shore of Lake Ontario.

One

FISHING CAMPS AND LAMPS

Association Island separates Lake Ontario, bottom, from Henderson Bay, top and right. This photograph is from the 1950s and shows a fully developed island community under GE ownership. At the right is the gravel bar leading to Hovey's Island and the mainland at Snowshoe Point.

Franklin S. Terry, left, and Burton G. Tremaine, owners of incandescent lamp companies in Chicago and Fostoria, Ohio, are waiting for a train in 1903. They discovered the beauty of Warner's Island during a fishing trip to Henderson Harbor in the same year. George H. Warner, proprietor of Warner's Inn of Henderson Harbor, owned the island. They wanted a location for their annual summer camp meetings to plan competition with their rival, General Electric. (Courtesy of WRHS.)

Terry and Tremaine and many other lamp company men stayed at the Colewood Cove campground on the western shore of Henderson Harbor during their 1903 and 1905 summer fishing trips. This c. 1900 photograph shows the campground, with a small building, flagpole, and several boats. It was on a farm owned by William C. and Elizabeth K. Butts. Because of heavy rain that made the men wet and miserable during their 1903 encampment at Colewood, they chose different camp locations the following summer.

From 1904 to 1906, dozens of lamp men, who had organized themselves as the National Electric Lamp Company (NELC), held most of their camp meetings at Chautauqua Lake in western New York State and the Muskoka Lakes and Montmorency Falls, Canada. Seated in the second row, located fifth, sixth, seventh, and eighth from the left, Henry A. Tremaine, Franklin S. Terry, John B. Crouse, and Burton G. Tremaine are the primary NELC and Association Island founders. Pictured in the background is Chautauqua Lake. (Courtesy of WRHS.)

The five lamp company men who organized the NELC and the 1906 purchase of Warner's Island are pictured in a scrapbook from their 1905 camp at Montmorency Falls, Quebec, Canada. From left to right are John B. Crouse, Franklin S. Terry, Burton G. Tremaine, Henry A. Tremaine, and J. Robert Crouse. Burton G. Tremaine had a connection to Henderson Harbor as the former Cleveland, Ohio, branch manager for the Agricultural Insurance Company of Watertown, New York. (Courtesy of WRHS.)

The summer camps for lamp company owners and managers from New York; Hartford, Connecticut; Boston, Massachusetts; Chicago, Illinois; St. Louis, Missouri; and Cleveland, Fostoria, and Shelby, Ohio, were similar to college fraternity gatherings, according to SUNY at Albany history professor Gerald Zahavi. Sporting events, such as this tug-of-war game at Chautauqua, baseball, archery, swimming races, gun shooting, and poker consumed their time when they were not planning competition against GE. These games would continue after the men organized Association Island. (Courtesy of WRHS.)

At the 1904 Chautauqua camp meeting, Sunbeam Lamp Company owner Franklin S. Terry entertained the men with his Victor Talking Machine and music from Italian tenor Enrico Caruso, Nellie Melba, Marcella Sembrich, and Henry Eames. The same tents pictured here would show up at Association Island a few years later. (Courtesy of WRHS.)

In 1905 and 1906, the NELC men returned to Henderson Harbor and camped again at Colewood, hidden behind the tree, top left. From their campsite, they could see Warner's Island across Henderson Bay, top right. Colewood was popular and often crowded. This may have inspired the NELC members to search for an exclusive and permanent campground. In this photograph from 1910 are sisters, from left to right, Thelma, Diantha, and Doris Evans and their cousin Dorothy Fish, rowing *Tin Boat* near Colewood. As of 2012, *Tin Boat* was still being used in the cove. (Courtesy of Dan Higgins.)

Bestow and Caroline Cooper Dexter, from nearby Roberts Corners in the town of Henderson, built the first summer cottage at Colewood in 1896. They named it Sleepy Hollow; it is pictured here in 1910 with extended members of the Dexter, Fish, and Evans families who summered in the cove. In 1927, William and Elizabeth Butts sold the campground lots to the Dexter, Fish, Evans, and Dunmore families. Except for their cottages, the first campground of the NELC men remains today in the same rustic condition as it was in 1903. (Courtesy of Dan Higgins.)

During the 1906 camp at Colewood, later spelled as Kohlwood, the lamp company owners agreed to purchase Warner's Island for $2,500. Prior to construction of the island boat lagoon, direct access to the island was from the southeastern shoreline; it was the only side deep enough for their double-ended rowing skiffs and naphtha launches, pictured here about 1906–1907.

Another early access point to Warner's Island was from nearby Hovey's or Snowshoe Island and Snowshoe Bay. In this c. 1915 photograph at Hovey's Landing in Snowshoe Bay, the *Wahine* is moored at the dock while a small launch is approaching the shore. Snowshoe Point is in the background. From Hovey's Island, visitors had to wade through shallow water on a gravel bar to reach Association Island.

Snowshoe Bay offered fishermen protected waters on their journey to Lake Ontario and the fishing shoals along Stony and Galloo Islands. Surrounded by mostly farm pasture with few cottages in 1906, fishing guides had to pull their double-ended rowing skiffs over the gravel bar between Snowshoe Point and Hovey's Island to get to the lake. This cumbersome task would be eliminated in 1927 with construction of the boat channel known as the Cut.

Henderson Harbor cottagers used Warner's Island for fishing and shore dinners, the midday meal during a fishing trip, consisting of fresh bass and perch caught in the morning and cooked over a campfire with potatoes and bacon. In this c. 1920 photograph, fish are in the frying pan along the southwest shore of Snowshoe Bay. The gravel bar to Hovey's Island is in the background. Many Association Island visitors were treated to a Henderson Harbor shore dinner. (Courtesy of John D. Marsellus.)

Before 1908, the NELC men had changed their name to National Electric Lamp Association (NELA) and renamed Warner's Island, Association Island. The striped tents they had used at Chautauqua, Muskoka, and Montmorency Falls were installed at Association Island. Plans were made for a boat lagoon, boathouses, dining hall, bathhouses, administration building, chapel, town hall, and hospital. The building in the background would later become the Black Catte Café.

The first dining hall at Association Island was actually a tent with a wooden floor. In this photograph from 1908, waiters, chefs, and kitchen staff pose in the dining tent with tables and chairs arranged for a large meal. All these items were purchased and shipped on boats to Association Island from Henderson Harbor. Most of the items remained on the island until they sold at auction 70 years later. (Courtesy of miSci.)

An early scrapbook shows, clockwise from top left, costumes for the School of Fish Club in 1909, the 1910 bathhouse, early meeting under the elm, original member "Governor" Pierce in 1909, NELA member N.L. Norris dressed as "Liza" in 1908, and rookies of 1912. (Courtesy of miSci.)

This 1908 image shows four early NELA men, including Burton G. Tremaine, left, with a catch of Lake Ontario black bass. The dining tent is in the background. At about this time, Terry and Tremaine began recruiting new NELA members by purchasing additional lamp companies. Deep in debt, they used GE money to expand the NELA and kept it a secret from the other members.

Renowned Henderson Harbor fishing guide Willett H. "Will" Stevens used Association Island for hunting and trapping prior to the arrival of the NELA men. Stevens and his brothers Alden and Albert were fishing guides for Association Island campers. Will Stevens was also the fishing guide for Secretary of State John W. Foster and his son-in-law Secretary of State Robert M. Lansing, who both had summer cottages across Henderson Bay from Association Island. Foster was secretary of state under Benjamin Harrison, and Lansing under Woodrow Wilson. (Courtesy of John Stevens.)

The Association Island boat lagoon had been constructed by 1908 for mooring the rowing skiffs, background left, and motorboats built by the Henderson Harbor Bassett family, right. The lagoon boathouse was built by 1909. Conditions on the island were still crude, however, because campers still slept in canvas tents, seen at right. Despite the few luxuries, such as electric lights and one bathhouse, Terry and Tremaine's initial invitations to GE executives to come to Association Island were rebuffed.

Harbor 1908
Association Island

Terry and Tremaine had convinced their rival company GE to invest a 75-percent stake in the NELC and kept it a secret from most everyone in the company. When the GE investors first came to Association Island, they stayed at the more refined Tyler's Inn, consisting, by the time of this photograph in 1910 of a party in the front lawn at Tyler's, of four buildings and a boathouse on the southeastern shore of Henderson Harbor.

The GE executives would leave Tyler's dock and boathouse in hired boats for meetings with the NELA leaders at the Colewood campgrounds, fishing shoals, or Association Island but they would return to Tyler's Inn each night. Most all campers would travel to Colewood campground by boat from Tyler's because a sturdy road through the Butts farm to the Colewood Cove was not built until after 1927.

The GE executives could comfortably wait for their boats in the screened second floor of Tyler's boathouse. Between 1908 and 1911, GE's money was fueling a NELA purchasing spree. Terry and Tremaine traveled the eastern half of the country, snapping up small lamp companies under the pretense of forming a larger NELA to better compete with GE. Terry later admitted in his memoirs that no one was told that GE was majority owner and providing the cash for buying more lamp companies.

A large motor launch, such as this moored at Tyler's dock around 1905, carried the GE and NELA men around Henderson Harbor and to Association Island. In the background on the right is a farm in the area known as Aspinwall Shores. The shoreline behind the boat would later become the Reed Canal area. Tyler's Inn and Marina maintained a link to Association Island until it was sold out of the Tyler family following World War II.

Two

GE TAKES OVER

By 1911, Franklin S. Terry, left, and Burton G. Tremaine, right, had developed NELA Park, the first suburban corporate industrial park in America, background, near Cleveland, which was funded by GE. 1911 was also the year the lamp manufacturers were sued for violation of the Sherman Antitrust Act. Following a consent decree, NELA was dissolved. In 1912, GE absorbed ownership of the lamp companies and Association Island.

GE continued the development of Association Island with substantial investment in island infrastructure. One of the first large buildings constructed was the administration building, foreground, where the porch and steps became a primary gathering place for campers.

GE also spent a sizeable amount of money furnishing new boats for the eight-slip boathouse over the island lagoon. The boathouse was necessary for the protection of the fleet of wooden boats and to haul them out of the water during northern New York winters. The second floor was a dance hall and movie theater. At right in this 1911 photograph are the first kitchen and the dining tent.

Another early view of the island lagoon with rowing skiffs, a small boathouse, and the rear of the large main boathouse in the background shows the elaborate facilities surrounding the docking area for boats. This area of the lagoon was used for smaller craft, which could fit beneath the stairs, left, that lead to the theater on the upper floor.

From Henderson Bay, this view of the island from about 1910 shows the large dining hall tent, left, and the first tent cabins with their canvas overhanging roofs. Also notable are the two large trees in the center. The tree on the left is the island's famous elm tree, which later would become the internationally recognized symbol of GE's Elfun Society, formed on the island in 1928. Both elm trees in this photograph were used for shade for Elfun meetings "under the elm."

Association Island, center, is pictured from Chestnut Ridge in Henderson Harbor in this photograph from the summer of 1909. The large boathouse had already been constructed, but the white canvas tents are visible, indicating that this photograph was taken before construction of the sleeping cabins. In the foreground along Harbor Road, the apple trees are from the Hugh and Minnie Gill apple orchard. On the right are Davis and Sixtown Islands.

A popular gathering spot for families to watch their children play at Association Island was from the steps of the administration building. There are many photographs and film scenes that depict families enjoying their children's sports activities on the parade ground at right. This photograph is from prior to 1920 because the cabins are made from canvas. The all-wood cabins would be built later.

GE often invited its star engineers and national celebrities to Association Island. Pictured from left to right on the steps of the original Association Island Administration Building, probably in September 1916, are GE's consultant wizard of electrical engineering and the developer of alternating current, Charles P. Steinmetz, and inventor of the light bulb, Thomas A. Edison. Edison arrived at the island with about 100 engineers from his company in New Jersey at the end of August 1916. This is the only known photograph of Edison at Association Island. (Courtesy of miSci.)

Swimming Dock, Association Island.   Henderson Harbor, N. Y.

Local carpenters constructed the large swim dock and slide platform on the east side of the island that extended into Henderson Bay. Different photographs over many years portray various swim platforms on the island. They were typically destroyed by winter ice, forcing them to be rebuilt.

The GE executives who spearheaded rapid development of Association Island into a full-scale company retreat and training center are pictured on the island in a c. 1925 photograph. Standing are, from left to right, GE vice presidents Burton G. Tremaine, Francis C. Pratt, and Franklin S. Terry. Sitting are, from left to right, GE chairman Owen D. Young, GE president Gerard Swope, and former GE president Edwin W. Rice Jr. (Courtesy of miSci.)

The GE Flying Courier was a Curtiss JN-4 "Jenny" biplane that flew daily to Association Island from GE headquarters in Schenectady, New York. The pilot, Victor A. Rickard, delivered newspapers and mail to campers at the island. This photograph is labeled "GE Air Service, Schenectady to Camp Lovejoy, Association Island, NY, September, 3–8, 1923." A film from this era shows Rickard landing this plane on the island, dropping off the mail, and taking off again. (Courtesy of Austin.)

In the 1920s, picnic lunches were held in the shade of a large elm tree on the southeast side of the island. In 1928, from a challenge by GE president Gerard Swope, the GE Elfun Society was organized under the elm tree. Originally a think tank and stock fund, the Elfun (Electric Funds) Society has grown to become one of the most charitable volunteer organizations in the world. A symbol of the Association Island elm tree still represents the Elfun Society today.

An early Association Island manager was John Austin, a New York City hotel and restaurant executive who moved his family to Henderson Harbor soon after World War I. Pictured on the island with his wife, Alice, in the early 1920s, Austin, during his 25 years as an island manager, amassed GE stock that was valued at a million dollars when his daughter Alice "Allie" Austin tendered the original paper certificates in the 1990s. Most of the proceeds were donated to charities. (Courtesy of Austin.)

John Austin managed the domestic staff and kitchen and dining hall employees. In this photograph from about 1923, Austin is sitting on the stool, with the kitchen staff. When Austin contracted an infection and had his leg amputated, the island staff presented him with a signed scrapbook in the early 1940s, which included this and many other Association Island photographs. (Courtesy of Austin.)

John Austin recruited many members of the Association Island kitchen staff from New York City for their expertise at cooking and service. While local women were also employed, it was typically those imported waitresses, like these pictured in the late-1920s in front of the dining hall, who worked the tables for the GE executives during meals and banquets on the island. (Courtesy of Austin.)

On arrival and departure days, campers would gather on the lagoon bulkhead for the ferryboats, such as the *Just Brown III*, pictured here on June 5, 1927. This is the only known photograph of this boat. The lagoon was three to five feet deep, with concrete walls embedded with steps for the passengers. The island marching band, at left along the shoreline, played for arrivals and departures. (Courtesy of Frank Bovee.)

Early rituals among GE employees included spirited competitions among the different company divisions. A march to a gathering would include the island's brass band and elaborate costumes. The sign in this early-1920s photograph indicates a chariot race and reads "Henderson Downs, Lost Business Derby, Four Races." The men are marching to the town hall. The administration building is on the left with the island elm tree above it, and the Black Catte Café is in the center with the chimney. (Courtesy of Austin.)

Costumes were part of the games and activities promoting competition among the different company divisions in manufacturing, sales, engineering, and management. In this photograph from the 1930s, the "Roaming Legion" is lined up with the "Nubians" for a sporting event on the island parade grounds. (Courtesy of miSci.)

In 1926, GE purchased nearby Hovey's Island from George S. Hovey, for $22,500. Also known a Snowshoe Island, it was turned into a golf course. The Hovey farmhouse, part of the Snowsho Inn, formerly operated by Winford J. "Winnie" and Martha Hovey, is in the background. (Courtes of miSci.)

Golfers in the late 1920s had to take a boat to Hovey's Island to continue their game after beginning on the first six holes that were on Association Island. From the former Hovey farmhouse porch, they could quench their thirsts. The amber-colored drinks in this photograph may be beer, which was readily available on the island during Prohibition. (Courtesy of miSci.)

Rum-running into Henderson Harbor increased in the late 1920s. Rum boats would cross Lake Ontario, top, from Canada and run into Snowshoe Bay, center, where they could unload Canadian beer, ale, and whiskey at farms, such as the Hovey's Island farm, top right, owned by GE. Claude and Clara Hovey's son Ken helped unload booze boats at their Dings Cove farm and boxes labeled "radio tubes" at Association Island that were filled with liquor.

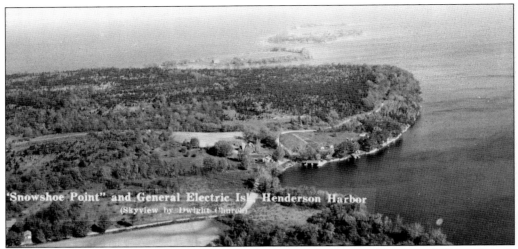

"Snowshoe Point" and General Electric Isl, Henderson Harbor
(Skyview by Dwight Church)

In this c. 1940 photograph, Dings Cove is at the bottom leading to Claude and Clara Hovey's Twin Elms Farm, located left of the double-slip boathouse. Snowshoe Point, which looks like a snowshoe, juts into Henderson Bay, and Hovey's, Association, Davis, and Sixtown Islands are at the top. The seclusion and deep water of Dings Cove in the 1920s and quick access to Snowshoe Road made it an ideal location for off-loading booze smuggled across the lake from Canada. (Courtesy of Church.)

Henderson Harbor moonshiners also sold whiskey to Association Island campers during Prohibition. Decorated Civil War veteran Jim Jackson, pictured with his wife, Phoebe, was arrested many times for operating an illegal still on the family farm at Sixtown Point near Association Island. Jackson lived to age 100, was reported to have shaken hands with Pres. Abraham Lincoln, and was reportedly present at Appomattox Courthouse, Virginia, to witness the surrender of Gen. Robert E. Lee. (Courtesy of Grover Moore.)

Three

DEPRESSION AND WORLD WAR II

By 1930, Association Island was nearly fully developed. The largest ferryboat, *Wahine*, was a familiar site around Henderson Harbor, carrying passengers back and forth to the island. In this 1930 scene, a cameraman is recording events of the day. Films of Association Island events from the 1920s to the 1950s were shown at GE meetings and venues throughout upstate New York. Henderson Harbor is in the distant background. (Courtesy of miSci.)

GE suspended operations at Association Island during the Great Depression. A small maintenance staff looked after the island, which by now included rows of sleeping cabins, boathouse, dining hall, administration building, town hall, hospital, bathhouses, Black Catte Café, and a power

generating station. This photograph shows Association Island, right, and Hovey's Island, left, along with Snowshoe Bay, Snowshoe Point, and the Stony Point Rifle Range, top left, and Stony and Galloo Islands in the top right background. (Courtesy of miSci.)

Lillian Tiller, of Belleville, New York, was 19 when she reported for work in the kitchen and dining hall at Association Island. Pictured in 1937 at the island boat landing, Tiller commuted to the island on the *Wahine* and would stay for the duration of a camp event. As Lillian Lattimer at the age of 94 in 2012, she recalled how she applied for the island job because her family's farmhouse on Tiller Road in Belleville had recently burned and they needed the money. (Courtesy of Lattimer.)

Manager John Austin hired Lillian Tiller. Austin was an accomplished New York City hotel and restaurant manager who worked for GE at Association Island for many years. Pictured in front of the *Wahine* in 1937, Austin was the father of the late Alice "Allie" Austin, a prominent resident of Henderson Harbor whose collection of island photographs and documents contributed to this book. (Courtesy of Lattimer.)

One of Lillian Tiller's many coworkers was Tommy Huttermann, a carpenter, pictured here constructing Association Island cabin No. 43 in 1937. One hundred sixty of these unique cabins were built. The overhanging roof, resembling the original canvas roof of earlier tent cabins, would be added to the front for additional shelter. (Courtesy of Lattimer.)

Lillian Tiller, who took many photographs during her stint on Association Island, spent most of her time working in the kitchen and dining hall preparing and serving meals. The kitchen was attached to the rear of the dining hall, and both were located near the large boathouse. The dining hall has been renovated and was being used as a conference center in 2012. (Courtesy of miSci.)

This 1946 scene inside the dining hall shows GE president Charles Wilson, seated second from the left, eating dinner after a late-evening arrival at Association Island. Note the abundance of windows facing the south and east to allow natural light to flood the dining hall. The china was stamped with the initials "A.I.C." for Association Island Corporation. (Courtesy of miSci.)

This large, two-story building is on the west side of Association Island, facing Hovey's Island and Lake Ontario. On the backside of the boat lagoon, it served as the employees' dormitory and bathhouse. Today, it serves as the office and store for the Association Island RV Resort and Marina. (Courtesy of miSci.)

The rear of the administration building in 1937 shows how large of a structure it was prior to being destroyed in a fire in 1946. Barely visible at the far left is the cabin that also burned in the fire. This side of the building faced the north and Lake Ontario while the other side overlooked the parade grounds and ball fields on the south and east side of the island, facing Henderson Bay. (Courtesy of Lattimer.)

The front of the eight-slip boathouse in 1937 shows how it was constructed within the boat lagoon. Initially, the walls of the bulkhead were wooden until concrete was added later. Note the Mobilgas pump. A 1914 magazine article reports that Standard Oil Company installed a gasoline pipeline from the mainland for boats on the island, but details of how this might have been accomplished are not given. (Courtesy of Lattimer.)

The stairs leading to the dance hall and theater on the second floor are visible on the far left of the boathouse. The lagoon walkway allowed pedestrians to move from the dining hall to the western side of the island without having to walk around the lagoon. In the early 1950s, the boathouse was torn down, according to the late Henderson resident Frank Ross, who was born on Association Island and whose father, Richard Ross, was island manager in 1940. (Courtesy of miSci.)

The slips in the front of the boathouse in 1937 show the four early wooden motor launches used at Association Island. They are, from left to right, the *Starling*, the *Snowshoe*, the *Claverack*, and the *Islander*. The boats' makers are unknown, but they appear to be of similar design and vintage. All were single-engine, inboard motor launches with a capacity of 15–18 passengers. (Courtesy of Lattimer.)

Island employee Bill Kendall is working on the roof of the *Wahine* in this photograph from 1937. The largest of the early island ferryboats, it was equipped with more than 40 life preservers, indicating its capacity for passengers. The *Wahine* was owned by the Island Transportation Company and carried passengers around Henderson Bay when not servicing Association Island. (Courtesy of Lattimer.)

The island town hall was designed as a combination meeting facility, theater with stage, and conference center. Events at the town hall often began with a ceremonial walk or parade to the building, constructed on the northern side of the island. The YMCA used it for similar activities in the 1960s. Listed as a historic building, the town hall was in a deteriorated state by 2012 but was scheduled for renovation. (Courtesy of miSci.)

The Black Catte Café was the bar and lunch hall attached to the golf clubhouse. Partly decorated with large cartoon cat characters, this was the party spot on the island after golf or tennis or for after-dinner drinks. This 1940 photograph shows the GE campers dressed in all white, probably for golf or a tennis tournament. (Courtesy of miSci.)

The late 1930s saw the revival of the sophomoric fraternity-style games and competitions among the different divisions within GE. At Camp Commercial in 1937, the "Cagey Captives, Knights of the Klunic" are lined up against the "Lonesome Eunuchs" for a competition ritual. The cage appears to be made from wood framing and large rubber tire tubes. The device on the right appears to be a luggage trailer. (Courtesy of miSci.)

Another example of the games between GE divisions at Camp Commercial in 1937 shows the men in bathing trunks of the period hauling what appears to be a chariot. It could be a trash hauler decorated for this particular event. Three of the men are wearing peach baskets on their backs. These competitions were used to inspire innovation and sales within the different GE divisions. (Courtesy of miSci.)

In 1930, the Association Island marching band is lined up in front of the dining hall for a photograph. The men are facing southeast and toward Henderson Bay. The band greeted island visitors, led ceremonial marches, played for moonlight cruises on the ferryboats, and performed opening and closing ceremonies each summer. (Courtesy of miSci.)

Having flown by seaplane from Schenectady in late June 1946, GE president Charles Wilson, right, arrives at Association Island with a GE vice president for Camp Engineering. This visit would prove to be one of the most eventful in just a few days. (Courtesy of miSci.)

Early on the morning of July 2, 1946, the iconic administration building burned to the ground. One cabin also burned because of its proximity to the administration building. Despite firefighting hoses stretching from underground water pipes and because local fire departments could not get to the island, the building was quickly consumed by the flames. Many records were lost. The end result was a fire truck and more firefighter training for island employees. The building in the background is the town hall. (Courtesy of miSci.)

Another view of the administration building fire shows the remains of the chimney and fireplace, papers and documents scattered on the lawn, hand-held firefighting equipment that was virtually useless, and the burned out shell of the cabin that was also consumed. The powerhouse and maintenance building is in the background. (Courtesy of miSci.)

In this photograph from later in 1946, looking west, the site of the former administration building is the lighter colored spot with an "X" walkway. Note the row of older cabins in the center right and the newer cabins built in the 1930s and 1940s at the bottom right. Hovey's Island is at the top left. The large open space in the middle includes the parade grounds and ball fields where the GE mail plane landed on the island in the 1920s. (Courtesy of miSci.)

In this view from the west end of the island looking east, the site of the former administration building is marked with the X-shaped landscaping feature above the powerhouse smokestack. The town hall is on the left; the large bathhouse/dormitory is in the center; the boathouse is out of the picture at the right. Uninhabited Sixtown Island, still owned by descendants of the Henderson Harbor Foster, Dulles, and Lansing families, is at the top left. (Courtesy of miSci.)

Gerard Swope, seen seated on the island in 1936, was GE president from 1922 to 1940 and the man credited with advocating full development of Association Island. Swope was the GE leader who, in 1928, issued a challenge to organize what later became the GE Elfun Society. It was founded on the Association Island lawn in the shade of a large elm tree. (Courtesy of miSci.)

From the 1950s, this photograph shows a meeting under the elm tree at Association Island. Prior to the spread of Dutch elm disease to northern New York in the 1960s, towering elm trees were ubiquitous at Henderson Harbor. The island elm also succumbed to the disease and was removed in the early 1970s. (Courtesy of miSci.)

In 1946, GE dedicated a World War II monument made from a large boulder with a bronze plaque. It was placed beneath the Association Island elm. It reserved this location in memory of the 1,335 GE men and women who gave their lives in World War II. In 2012, the boulder was still on the island but toppled over and missing the plaque. (Courtesy of miSci.)

After closing during World War II, Association Island reopened in the summer of 1946 with GE refocused on sales to the baby-boom generation. Celebrities, authors, and motivational speakers were invited to the island camps. Although unidentified, the man in the center in this June 1946 photograph is getting VIP transportation to the island on the *Islander*. Note the wicker chairs, the heavy canvas rain cover, and Henchen Marina at Henderson Harbor in the background. (Courtesy of miSci.)

GE's Association Island was in a remote section of northern New York State. Visitors traveled by train, car, or boat. When it was time to leave the island, campers had to check in with the island's New York Central Railroad ticket office. Tickets were issued and stamped at the island because the local train stations were just small whistle stops. (Courtesy of miSci.)

Four

GLORY DAYS OF THE 1950s

A copy of this early-1950s aerial photograph, from the GE Grumman Mallard seaplane, hung on the wall at Henchen Marina in Henderson Harbor for many years. The photograph was taken soon after the large eight-slip boathouse in the island lagoon was torn down. Age and ice jams may have taken their toll on the boathouse. The larger boats such as the *Elsie M.*, *Claverack II*, *Islander II*, and *Spirit of the Island*, anchored in the bay, could not fit into the slips. (Courtesy of miSci.)

Inside of the boat lagoon in the early 1950s, the new gas dock, right, replaced the large boathouse. Several vintage runabouts are docked in the background, including Lymans and a Chris-Craft. GE's Grumman Mallard seaplane is parked at the shoreline. (Courtesy of miSci.)

Another view of the gas dock in 1956 shows the *Spirit of the Island* cruiser and two runabouts that were used for fishing and water skiing. The employees' dormitory is in the right background. This building is still standing and is presently used as the office and store for Association Island RV Park and Marina. (Courtesy of miSci.)

50

The island engineering department was a small barn in front of the power plant and smokestack, center background. All of these structures are gone. Pictured, from left to right, are a 1940s bicycle, the island's Willys-Jeep truck used to cross the gravel bar from Hovey's Island, and a 1930s fire truck. (Courtesy of miSci.)

The Association Island engineering and maintenance crew was made up of men from surrounding communities in 1954. Although all of these men cannot be identified, several Henderson Harbor area residents are among them. They include, second from the left, Carl Roof; fourth from the left, Joe DeLaVergne; and sixth from the left, Albert "Nook" Miles. Sitting tenth from the left is Nicholas Casario, and at the far right is Keith Hughes. Crouching at the far right is Mac Whitney. (Courtesy of miSci.)

The Association Island boat crew was at its peak in the 1950s. Crew members are pictured in Henderson Harbor in front of the island's largest ferryboats, the *Islander II* and *Claverack II*, with Ike, a dog named after Pres. Dwight D. Eisenhower. They include, from left to right, (first row) James Lynch, Norman P. Seymour Sr., Robert E. Pratt, Dean Golden, and Robert Walker Sr.; (second row) third and fourth from the left, Mack Agaciewski and Maynard Shutts. (Courtesy of miSci.)

Visitation and entertainment was also at its peak in the early 1950s. Although postwar management styles were becoming decentralized within GE, invitations to Association Island were still coveted by managers because they provided a chance to meet and mingle with the top corporate executives. In this undated photograph, the island boathouse is still standing and is pictured from a scenic overlook on New York State Route 3.

Most Association Island visitors arrived by train to stations along the New York Central tracks. They were bused from the small train stations to Henderson Harbor for their boat ride to the island. In this photograph from the early 1950s, the *Claverack II* and *Spirit of the Island* have just returned campers to the GE passenger dock to board Greyhound buses for their return trip home. This view is from Harbor View Road looking across Harbor Road in Henderson Harbor. (Courtesy of miSci.)

Luggage, golf clubs, and other large items were carried to Association Island from the GE freight dock on the barge *Elsie* M. This site along lower Harbor Road was the former Hamm and Hovey coal, feed, and lumber dock. It later became Bob's Landing and Restaurant. Today, the earthen wharf remains, but the two-story building is gone. (Courtesy of miSci.)

On arrival days, Henderson Harbor was packed with parked cars, and passengers lined up to board the ferryboats for Association Island. In this early-1950s scene at the former Harbor Inn dock, all but one visitor have removed their ties. Visitors caught wearing a tie at Association Island were tossed into the lagoon in a ritualistic hazing designed to encourage visitors to dress down and relax. (Courtesy of miSci.)

Arrivals and departures at Association Island were often marked with elaborate flag-raising or -lowering ceremonies and speeches. Gathered on the parade grounds around the flagpole in matching caps and jackets in this mid-1950s photograph, GE managers listened to speeches from top executives and offered salutes to the American and GE flags as the island brass band played patriotic songs. (Courtesy of miSci.)

Luggage was transported to Association Island on the *Elsie M.* and then hauled to individual cabins in the island's Willys-Jeep truck. Many local college students found summer employment at Association Island, such as this group of young men in 1954. The island cabins are on both sides of the tree-lined concrete path on the northwestern shore of the island. (Courtesy of miSci.)

The full-time maintenance crew and part-time summer landscaping crew kept the Association Island grounds in pristine condition. Many college students competed for the jobs and the chance to spend their summer on the island with a room at the employees' dormitory. This photograph from the early 1950s shows one of the island's Willys-Jeep vehicles. (Courtesy of miSci.)

A close-up view of the architecturally unique Association Island cabins shows the distinctive overhanging roof in this scene from the early 1950s. Local carpenters built 160 of these cabins. Henderson resident James Golden, son of ferryboat captain Dean Golden, remembers cleaning many of these cabins for painting in 1953. It would have been the last major renovations to the cabins before GE left the island in 1956. The cabins were sold at auction in the mid-1970s and removed from the island. (Courtesy of miSci.)

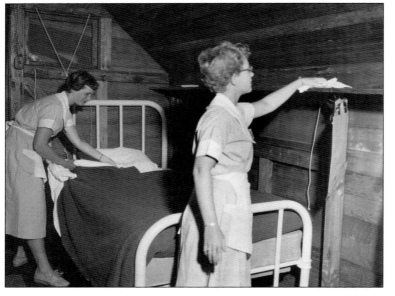

Each of the cabins was cleaned and outfitted with new linens for each group of camp visitors. Dozens of local women worked on the cleaning staff, making beds and preparing each cabin for new visitors. At left, Ellisburg, New York, resident Eleanor Eastman is making a cabin bed while another worker cleans a shelf in one of the rustic cabins. (Courtesy of miSci.)

At first glance, it appears the kitchen staff is peeling potatoes. However, these are members of the Association Island landscaping crew cleaning golf balls. In 1954, campers frequented the island driving range, which had replaced six holes on the former island golf course. Many campers whacked golf balls into Henderson Bay. Many balls were recovered, cleaned with detergent, teed up, and whacked into the bay again. (Courtesy of miSci.)

Association Island campers ate and drank as if they were in a first-class restaurant. An island picnic chef displays three-inch-thick steaks ready for the grill in the summer of 1954. The dining hall and kitchen are in the background. Campers often took their dinner on the lawn beneath the Association Island elm tree, overlooking Henderson Bay. (Courtesy of miSci.)

A sizeable infirmary-hospital was constructed in 1909–1910 on the northeast side of the island. During peak summer months, it had a large medical staff, such as the group photographed here in the 1950s. One of the oldest buildings on the island, the hospital is now a bathhouse and recreation center for the Association Island RV Resort and Marina. (Courtesy of miSci.)

The town hall doubled as the island stage and movie theater, especially after the boathouse, which included a theater, was torn down. In this early-1950s photograph, a projectionist is preparing for an evening movie at the Association Island Town Hall. The ventilation pipes on the slide and movie projectors indicates the heat produced by the high intensity lamps. (Courtesy of miSci.)

Association Island had its own public address system for music and announcements. The mixing box and turntables in this photograph are state of the art for the early 1950s. Speakers were mounted on poles and tree limbs throughout the island. Many Henderson Harbor residents recall hearing soothing music from Association Island during warm and still summer nights in the 1940s and 1950s. (Courtesy of miSci.)

This early-1950s photograph of a utility room at Association Island does not look like much but it was an elaborate electricity generating system. Generators were used on the island prior to electrical wires being strung from Hovey's Island and the mainland to Association Island in the early 1960s. Years later, the YMCA sold the generators for income. (Courtesy of miSci.)

GE mid-level managers may have arrived by boat, but top executives and VIP's often arrived at Association Island in the company seaplane. In the early 1950s, it was a Grumman Mallard, 10-passenger seaplane that would land on the eastern side of Association Island and taxi up a ramp to an apron near the boat lagoon. After it was sold, this plane crashed in 1986 with loss of life in the Bahamas and was scrapped. (Courtesy of miSci.)

A softball game was almost always underway at Association Island in the 1940s and 1950s. Played on the parade grounds in the middle of the island, the games were ideally located for campers to sit under their cabin overhanging roofs and watch the games. When company meetings were completed in the mornings, sporting events would begin immediately following lunch. (Courtesy of miSci.)

Six holes for golfing were on the northern side of the island, but campers often lined up on the parade grounds for a driving range. The extra holes on Hovey's Island had been converted to other uses by the 1950s. Well into the 1970s, storage sheds on the island were filled with bags of old golf clubs, left on the island by players who never returned. (Courtesy of miSci.)

The shuffleboard court was situated along the walkway from the dining hall to the first row of cabins. The small mound of flowers at the end of the walkway marked the location of the former administration building, which burned in 1946. The golf driving range is in the background, and the original row of sleeping cabins extends as far as can be seen to the northeast side of the island. (Courtesy of miSci.)

Sailing on Henderson Bay was also a favorite pastime for island campers. Most of them were novice sailors who learned the craft while at the island. This photograph is from 1954 and displays some of the single-mast, retractable-keel sailboats provided for campers. On Monday, July 20, 1931, the island's first death occurred when a prominent GE engineer drowned when his sailboat capsized during a squall on the bay between Henderson Harbor and the island. As a result, a motor launch was assigned to cruise among all island sailing activities in future years. (Courtesy of miSci.)

Archery on Association Island may have made visitors feel like they were at a children's summer camp. The author recalls finding dozens of bows and hundreds of arrows packed away in boxes on the island in the early 1970s. The rear of the Black Catte Café is in the background of this early-1950s photograph. (Courtesy of miSci.)

trap and skeet shooting range was situated on the northeast end of the island so the shot could
e propelled over Henderson Bay. In this early-1950s photograph, range supervisor Mac MacCowell,
ft, helps retired GE vice president Roy Muir of Schenectady steady his aim. Note how far away
om the sleeping cabins the shooting range is situated. (Courtesy of miSci.)

lso on the secluded northeast end of the island was the live-bird tower shooting range. Highly
ntroversial in 2012, this sport was popular among professional men in the 1940s and 1950s.
ive birds were released from the small door at the top of the tower as shooters took aim. The
ast side of Sixtown Island is in the right background. (Courtesy of miSci.)

Bass and perch were plentiful on the rocky shoals around Association Island. Most often, however, island campers hired a seasoned Henderson Harbor fishing guide for a trip to the offshore island fishing hot spots of eastern Lake Ontario. Displaying the day's catch on the island fish board was a tradition that continues today on Association Island and in Henderson Harbor. (Courtesy of miSci.)

Henderson Bay waters were typically cold, even during the summer months. Anchoring a barge on the eastern side of the island in the early 1950s created an ideal location for sunbathing. Note the lifeguard and the long swimming dock. The water in this part of Henderson Bay is from three to eight feet deep with a rocky bottom. (Courtesy of miSci.)

f the weather cooperated, dinners were held under the Association Island elm tree on the eastern ide of the island, facing Henderson Bay. In this early-1950s scene, the dining hall wooden tables and chairs have been carried to the lawn. The island elm tree is at the left. (Courtesy of miSci.)

Association Island ampers were also ntertained at night. Song and dance roupes, like this one n a risqué display or the early 1950s, erformed on an utdoor stage. Some erformances were rganized among the ampers, but this vent is likely from a raveling group from ne of the larger cities n New York State. Courtesy of miSci.)

Whether it was for an Elfun Society meeting, a speech, or a training session given by a GE executive, the large gathering location on the island in good weather was under the island elm tree. This early-1950s scene appears to be a chance for campers to ask questions of the speaker.

eft. He is standing at the large World War II memorial boulder and plaque. The island elm tree s just out of the picture at the left. (Courtesy of miSci.)

The *Spirit of the Island* leaving the Association Island dock at the end of summer in 1956 was symbolic of GE pulling out of Association Island. A sleek pleasure cruiser, often piloted by Capt. Robert E. Pratt, this elegant Richardson boat embodied the style and magnificence of GE's presence in Henderson Harbor. The island was expensive to maintain, and as a result, when GE left, there began a gradual but long and steady economic decline for the surrounding community. (Courtesy of miSci.)

When the island's large boathouse was torn down in the early 1950s, more room was provided in the lagoon for the larger ferryboats such as the *Islander II* and *Claverack II*. This scene is from 1956, the final year for GE at Association Island. On the right is the dining hall with the kitchen directly behind it. Note the window vents in the kitchen roof. In the far background is the island engineering barn. (Courtesy of miSci.)

Loaded with passengers for the return trip to Henderson Harbor, the *Islander II* is making one of its final voyages across Henderson Bay in the summer of 1956. Most of the passengers aboard the boat in this photograph would never return. GE pulled out of Association Island after 1956 and repositioned its management training activities to Crotonville, New York. (Courtesy of miSci.)

The final voyage of the *Islander II* was given a send-off cheer and a song from an island band and choir. Several original songs were written and performed specifically for Association Island from the 1920s through this event in the summer of 1956. Behind the choir, musicians are playing the accordion and a bass fiddle. A stand microphone is sending the music through the island's public address system. After 1956, the *Islander II* was sold, but its twin ferryboat, the *Claverack*, remained on the island into the early 1970s. (Courtesy of miSci.)

The former Harbor Inn dock was the busiest location in Henderson Harbor on arrival and departur day for Association Island campers. In this early-1950s scene, the *Claverack II* is moored at th dock while the *Elsie* M. plies the harbor for the GE freight dock farther down Harbor Road. Th tent behind the trees is located about where the front of the original Harbor Inn looked out ov Henderson Harbor.

GE contracted with Greyhound Bus Lines to transport Association Island campers between th New York Central train stations in Adams, Adams Center, and Pierrepont Manor, New York. Th parking lot in Henderson Harbor, filled with buses in 1956, is the site of the original Harbor In The concrete bulkhead and railing on the left are part of the original steps that led from Harb Road down to the entrance of the four-story Harbor Inn. (Courtesy of miSci.)

Five

YMCA and Recreation

n September 15, 1959, GE donated Association Island to the New York State YMCA. The value the island properties was estimated at $250,000. The full-market value of Association and Hovey's ands in 2012 was estimated by the Jefferson County tax assessor at $4,590,000. Pictured, from ottom to top are, the tip of Hovey's Island, Association Island, Davis Island, Sixtown Island, ll Island, Bass Island, and, in the far distance, Horse Island. (Courtesy of miSci.)

The GE property donated to the YMCA included 146 acres. Association Island, center, was 64 acres. Hovey's Island, right, was 34 acres, and the rest of the land was on Snowshoe Point. Sixtown and Davis Islands, left, were not part of the holdings. The YMCA planned to use the facilities for a leadership training camp, state conventions and conferences, and youth summer camps. (Courtesy of miSci.)

The New York State YMCA appointed Richard W. Billings, left, director of the summer camp at Association Island. Pictured here with consultant H. Kaye Kerr, center, of Syracuse and Henderson Harbor, and William "Bill" Foster, technical engineer at the island, Billings moved his family to neighboring Hovey's Island in 1960 and, along with his wife, Jill, transformed Association Island into an elaborate YMCA summer camp. (Courtesy of Billings.)

This is the view from Hovey's Island looking northeast across the gravel bar to Association Island about 1960. When the water level in Lake Ontario was low, visitors could walk across the bar. After electric wires had been strung across the bar, on July 14, 1964, 21-year-old David Erickson was electrocuted when his sailboat mast came into contact with the wires. Further adding to the tragedy, his four-year-old brother Craig Erickson drowned off the family's Henderson Harbor motel dock a week later.

Drive from "Snowshoe Point" to Y.M.C.A. Island, (Lake Ontario at Henderson Harbor, New York.)

The YMCA took over a fully developed Association Island with tremendous financial and maintenance obligations. This map, redrawn by artist Emily Anthony from an original island map, shows the scope of island development. When the YMCA assumed ownership, the administration building had been lost to fire and the large boathouse had been torn down.

The YMCA struggled with the cost of operating ferryboats. YMCA employees from Henderson Harbor were often carried across the gravel bar in this Willys-Jeep truck, obtained during the GE sale. Driving the truck in this c. 1960 photograph is Albert "Nook" Miles, owner of the Gill House in Henderson Harbor. In the back are island employees Carl B. Roof, Florence Babcock, Nicholas Cassario, and Alvin Whitney, among others. (Courtesy of Billings.)

The YMCA installed a permanent causeway from Hovey's Island to Association Island in 1968. Despite regular maintenance with bulldozers, it washed away several times until it was fortified with heavier gravel from the DeWitt Hubbard farm in Henderson in 1972. Visitors could drive across the bridge known as the Cut, linking Snowshoe Point and Hovey's Island, and then to Association Island via the causeway. The fleet of island boats was gradually reduced to a few fishing and pleasure launches. (Courtesy of Billings.)

The YMCA focused on leadership training and sports camps at Association Island during the 1960s. Campers arrived from all over New York State. This group of young women in the mid-1960s is listening to a sports instructor in front of the Association Island Town Hall, the same building in which GE campers held their morning business meetings. (Courtesy of Billings.)

YMCA campers are playing a game of volleyball on the floor of the large Association Island Town Hall and theater in the 1960s. This is one of a few photographs of the inside of the town hall known to exist. Note the high ceilings and the velvet curtain across the stage. The town hall was in very poor condition in 2012 but it was listed as a historic landmark and is scheduled for renovation by the island owners. (Courtesy of Billings.)

For income, the YMCA rented facilities at Association Island for weddings and corporate meetings. On July 3, 1965, Henderson resident Grover Moore married Carol Fishel, both right, and they held their wedding reception in the Association Island dining hall. Both had worked at Association Island in previous years, and Moore is a descendant of Jim Jackson, the Civil War veteran profiled in chapter 2. (Courtesy of Grover Moore.)

YMCA campers continued the Association Island tradition of lunch on the lawn just outside the dining hall. The longest row of sleeping cabins is in the background, and limbs from the island elm tree can be seen on the right. In this mid-1960s view, the island's wicker and wooden chairs have been replaced by folding metal chairs, but the original wooden dining tables are still being used. (Courtesy of Billings.)

In this 1960s promotional photograph for the YMCA, the identities of the women participating in a tennis lesson on Association Island could not be determined. In the background are, from right to left, the rear of Ontario Lodge, which was a motel-style dormitory, and the first bathhouse built on piers, built prior to 1910. Both buildings remained on the island in 2012 but in poor condition. (Courtesy of Billings.)

In the 1960s, many Henderson Harbor residents continued their seasonal employment with the YMCA, as they had with GE, at Association Island. In the island kitchen, Nadine Roof Shutts, center, whose husband Maynard Shutts worked on the GE ferryboats, is helping coworkers prepare desserts for a summer meal. (Courtesy of Billings.)

In the 1960s, the YMCA utilized the Black Catte Café as a breakfast and lunch counter. The women in this promotional photograph could not be identified except for Marilyn Billings, third from left. The Black Catte Café interior was decorated in elaborate woodwork and a large fieldstone fireplace. It is still used today by the Association Island RV Resort and Marina. (Courtesy of Billings.)

Financial hardship forced the YMCA to leave Association Island in 1966 and sell an option on the property to private developers in September 1968 for a reported $300,000. However, a large cottage and marina development proposal, which also included Hovey's Island and Snowshoe Bay, pictured here, failed to win approval. Various plans for private or public ownership and use of the islands were debated until March 1973, when the nonprofit Association Island Recreational Corporation (AIRC), directed by Richard W. Billings, purchased the property for $310,000. (Courtesy of miSci.)

This photograph shows the proximity of Association Island, top left, to Henderson Harbor. Richard W. Billings spent hundreds of hours attempting to maintain the island as a nonprofit venture for the public use for residents of Henderson and Henderson Harbor. With the AIRC arts and crafts members Jill Billings, Richard and Sally Stevens, Julie Lake Bettinger, and Lila Bull, Billings organized visits by symphony, theater, and arts and cultural groups. However, financial issues were simply overwhelming.

Local citizens were invited to Association Island events, and many Henderson Harbor residents traveled to the island in their boats. In this photograph from the early 1970s, several Henderson Harbor fishing boats are moored in the island lagoon along with the *Claverack II*. (Courtesy of Julie West.)

Association Island was also opened to the public for fundraising events. In September 1970, the Henderson Area Association organized an ox roast on the island, and 1,200 people who contributed money for an environmental clean-up program for Lake Ontario attended it. Association member Ralph Kohl is carving the barbequed ox in this photograph from the *Jefferson County Journal*.

During the ox roast fundraisers, Henderson area families played sports events on the same fields enjoyed by GE families. This photograph from September 2, 1970, shows a softball game underway, and the Association Island Town Hall, in very good condition, is in the background. Henderson resident Paul Shutts is the boy walking along the path. His parents, Maynard and Nadine Shutts, both worked at Association Island. (Courtesy of Julie West.)

The first fundraiser by the Henderson Area Association drew hundreds of families to Association Island for the ox roast, music from bands, and sports events, such as this volleyball game near the island's Elfun Square. In the background of this September 2, 1970, photograph are the skeletal remains of the island elm tree and the World War II memorial monument. The island dining hall is at the far right, and Henderson Harbor is in the background. (Courtesy of Julie West.)

After five years as an environmental, arts, and cultural center, the AIRC hosted the US Sailing Center including windsurfing championships and training programs for the US Olympic Sailing Team. This photograph from the 1950s indicates there was always a stiff wind in Henderson Bay around Association Island. After sailors trained at Association Island for the 1976 Olympics, the island was abandoned until it reopened in 2002 as the Association Island RV Resort and Marina. (Courtesy of miSci.)

Six

BOATS

One of the first large boats devoted to servicing Association Island was the *Dauntless* in 1912. The 80-foot gasoline-converted steamer is pictured at the Harbor Inn dock soon after its arrival. It could carry more than 50 campers to Association Island. Snow's Hotel was sold by proprietor Goodwin M. Snow to Charles J. Purdy in 1912, when it was renamed the Harbor Inn. Purdy had sold his Philadelphia lamp manufacturing company to the NELA in 1909 for $35,000.

A steamer that plied the waters of Henderson Harbor is moored at the Harbor Inn dock about 1912–1913. Dozens of the GE men attended camps at the same time, so large boats, such as this one, were needed to ferry them across the harbor to Association Island. Note the double-ended rowing skiffs, the Harbor Inn flag, and the pleasant sitting area at the front of the dock.

Sailboats and cruisers crowd Henderson Harbor in this 1927 photograph, taken from Pilon's Dock, a boat livery owned by Fred and Doris Pilon and the former site of Snow's Garage and Ontario Grocery. The large cruiser on the left was part of the Association Island fleet. Colewood Cove is in the right background.

Although slightly out of focus, this 1937 photograph shows Association Island employee Bill Brabant carrying a line on Pilon's Dock in Henderson Harbor. Note the sleek wooden launches on the right, the boardinghouse in the background, and the sign with the partial word advertising beer. This location later became the new Harbor Inn. (Courtesy of Lattimer.)

This photograph from Pilon's Dock in Henderson Harbor shows Joel Wescott, left, and Fred J. "Jupie" Pilon Jr. at the helm of a cabin cruiser in the early 1940s. White's Bay is in the background. Wescott is from the last of the farm families who lived on Stony Island. They moved off the island in the late 1930s. Wescott's relatives sold their northeast Henderson Bay farm to New York State for Wescott's Beach State Park. (Courtesy of Joel Wescott.)

Association Island boats shared Henderson Bay with well-known sailing craft such as E. Austin Barnes's large yawl *Themis*, pictured in the 1920s. Barnes and his wife, Eva Snaith Barnes, purchased Henderson Harbor's Paradise Park Hotel for their summer cottage in the 1920s. From there, Barnes had to navigate the *Themis* around Association Island at Lime Barrel Shoal to get into the deep waters of Lake Ontario. The shoreline of Colewood Cove is on the right.

A Bassett-built boat that made regular trips around Association Island from Henderson Harbor was *Eunice*, owned by Ray H. Wescott Sr. of Stony Island and Henderson Harbor and named for his wife. Pictured at Stony Island with Galloo Island in the background, this is the kind of boat that early visitors to Association Island used for fishing over the shoals in eastern Lake Ontario. (Courtesy of Joel Wescott.)

Boats in Henderson Harbor during the 1920s included this barrel-back runabout, right, and a Bassett-built launch, left. These boats are pictured in this c. 1925 photograph at a well-known boathouse along Harbor Road next to Tyler's Inn that was still in use as of 2012. The boathouse and neighboring cottage, across Henderson Harbor from the Colewood campground, have been owned successively by the Stillman, Junker, and Kerr families over more than 100 years. (Courtesy of John Ash Clark.)

The *Islander* slides into the Association Island lagoon loaded with passengers from Henderson Harbor in 1937. The island brass band is on the lagoon breakwater to greet them. The *Islander* and its matching boats, the *Snowshoe* and *Claverack*, arrived at the island in the 1920s.

The *Islander* is unloading passengers from the stern in 1930 for Camp Engineering. Note the wood and canvas bumpers placed along the concrete bulkhead of the lagoon. Large pirate and Indian facades greeted the GE island visitors that summer. They addressed the theme of the activities for the week. At the far right is a Mobilgas pump used to refuel the boats. (Courtesy of miSci.)

The most recognized boat from Association Island in the 1920s and 1930s was the *Wahine*, pronounced as "wah-heen." Association Island employee Larry Garnsey is posing on the bow of the large ferryboat in this photograph from 1937. The *Wahine* was initially owned by Harbor Inn proprietor Charles J. Purdy and was contracted to run a triangular route between Sackets Harbor, Henderson Harbor, and Association Island during the summer. (Courtesy of Lattimer.)

Another view of the *Wahine* shows the boat ready to discharge passengers at the Association Island dock for Camp General in 1936. The *Wahine* was also used for midnight harbor cruises with the island band playing popular songs such as "Harbor Lights" as it cruised along the Henderson Harbor shoreline in 1937. (Courtesy of miSci.)

Also arriving for Camp General in the summer of 1936 is a VIP aboard the *Miss St. Lawrence II*. Although the man getting off the boat is unidentified, GE hosted many motivational speakers, celebrities, and business consultants at the island. The bow of the original *Snowshoe* can be seen at the left, and the island boathouse is in the background. (Courtesy of miSci.)

Some visitors cruised to Association Island in their own pleasure yachts. This large cabin cruiser is tied to the Harbor Inn dock in 1937 waiting for a trip to Association Island. Cruisers could navigate to Henderson Harbor from as far away as Toronto, Canada, and Buffalo, New York, and from the Thousand Islands. Note the two lanterns hanging from the power pole in the background. (Courtesy of Lattimer.)

In the 1930s, Eleanor Lansing Dulles is sailing the family's Ackroyd dingy, the *Scud*, in Henderson Bay, with Association Island in the background on the left. Her family's Sixtown Island is on the right. She was named for her uncle, former secretary of state Robert M. Lansing. Her brothers were future secretary of state John Foster Dulles and future CIA director Allen Welsh Dulles, and her grandfather was former secretary of state John W. Foster. Dr. Eleanor Dulles later distinguished herself as head of the State Department's West German desk following World War II. The *Scud* was donated to the Antique Boat Museum in Clayton, New York. (Courtesy of Mary Parke Manning.)

Meag 12 07   Published by Mrs. Nellie E. Warriner.

Mrs N E Cooper I do not need a Stenographer I have not business enough for one Thanks for your kindness G H Warner

Sailboats and rowboats were used by visitors to Warner's Inn, pictured on the left, in 1907. Situated with a sunset view across Henderson Bay to Association Island, Warner's Inn was adjacent to the Foster, Lansing, and Dulles cottages, on the right, where the family summer compound was still occupied in 2012 by Dr. Mary Parke Edwards Manning and family.

When GE pulled out of Association Island, its docking space at the former Harbin Inn, located on the right behind the trees in the background, remained vacant for several years and was used as a swimming hole by Henderson Harbor kids. Later, it was developed into a yacht basin for sailboats and has remained in use as a boatyard since. In this c. 1960 photograph, two large cruisers are moored in the former GE basin at Henderson Harbor.

The *Wahine* was the largest of the early ferryboats running to Association Island. Its final disposition could not be determined, but various newspaper articles describe how Association Island boats were sold over time to make room for newer and larger boats. In this 1937 photograph from Camp Engineering, the *Wahine* has just arrived at the island. Note the large stack of life preservers, amidships. (Courtesy of miSci.)

In the 1940s, the *Rose Ann II* delivered passengers between Henderson Harbor and Association Island. In this photograph from the late 1940s, several men are arriving at the island on the 28-foot Richardson cruiser. The man at the right with his hand on another man's back appears to be GE executive Charles Wilson. (Courtesy of miSci.)

One of the most beautiful boats in the Association Island fleet was the *Spirit of the Island*, a 30-foot cruiser that appeared in the 1940s and was passed on to the YMCA in the 1960s. In this photograph, it is registered in 1950 with Capt. Robert E. Pratt at the helm. This boat was likely used for VIP transportation to and from the island. Looking northeast, Henderson Bay toward Sackets Harbor is in the background. (Courtesy of miSci.)

Another sleek Henderson Harbor boat was a 36-foot cabin cruiser custom made for Marsellus Casket Company owner John C. Marsellus, whose cottage looked out over Henderson Bay and Association Island. The *Rijobe*, named for the Marsellus children, Richard, John, and Betty, was an ideal lake boat for all kinds of weather. In this photograph from the 1940s, it is run onto the stone beach of Sixtown Island next to Association Island. (Courtesy of John D. Marsellus.)

US Coast Guard boats patrolled the waters around Association Island from bases at Big Sandy or Galloo Island, and later, from Sackets Harbor. This Coast Guard surfboat, stationed at Galloo Island, west of Association Island, would have been a familiar vessel to the campers in the early 1950s. The Coast Guard also ran regular patrols around Association Island during Prohibition. (Courtesy of NCNYCGA.)

Association Island maintained a fleet of small sailboats for campers. Lessons were given to novice sailors, and after the tragic drowning of a GE engineer in one of these sailboats in 1931, powerboats were assigned to cruise among the sailors. Association Island is in the left background, and the eastern tip of Sixtown Island is in the far background of this early 1950s photograph. (Courtesy of miSci.)

naller craft were sometimes used to carry passengers between regular ferry schedules. On board e *Nancy J.* in 1954, four GE managers are leaving the island for Henderson Harbor. The original olewood Cove NELC campground site is in the far background.

s attendance at Association Island expanded, larger boats were needed. The *Claverack* and *lander* were replaced by the *Claverack II* and *Islander II*. In this 1950s view, the *Claverack II* is aving the island dock loaded with passengers for Henderson Harbor. This boat remained in use n the island into the early 1970s. (Courtesy of miSci.)

The fate of the *Islander II* is unknown, but it disappeared from the GE fleet sometime between 1957 and 1960. Capt. Robert E. Pratt is posing for a 1956 photograph on the stern of the empty boat in the middle of Henderson Harbor. The former Colewood Cove campground, Highland Park, and Paradise Park are in the background. (Courtesy of miSci.)

The Association Island landing barge, *Elsie M.*, usually carried luggage, golf clubs, food and drinks, and even vehicles to the island. In this photograph from the early 1950s, it is loaded with passengers. The *Elsie M.* used the GE freight dock along Harbor Road in Henderson Harbor. (Courtesy of miSci.)

The GE freight dock was nearly across Henderson Harbor from the Colewood Cove campground, as seen just above the middle car, the origin of the Association Island concept. This early-1950s photograph shows the *Elsie M.* ready to load a vehicle or supplies for the island. The sign on the two-story freight house on the right reads "General Electric Freight Dock."

This view looks southeast from the GE freight dock along the Harbor Road shoreline. From about 1950, this photograph shows a sleek plywood launch tied off at bow and stern. Tyler's Inn is in the background directly above the end of the dock, and the Sealright Corporation's Henderson Harbor property for access to Stony Island is directly above the boat.

The *Hullaballoo* was a 23-foot Lyman Islander whose misspelled name was for lyrics in a popular Association Island song from the 1920s. It went, "Hullabaloo, Hullabaloo, we're going to have a happy Hullabaloo. The island, the island, they want us to work and to play. To hell with the work we say. We're going to have a happy Hullabaloo." Also at the island lagoon in this 1950s photograph are the *Wahine II* and the *Elsie M.* The island chorus is performing at right. (Courtesy of miSci.)

One of the final GE boat departures in the summer of 1956 is portrayed in this photograph from the island lagoon. The *Wahine II* is loading passengers while still utilizing wicker chairs in the stern. The *Claverack II* is off-loading supplies to the flatbed truck while waiting to move into the passenger loading side of the dock. Within weeks of when this photograph was taken, GE would be gone from Association Island. (Courtesy of miSci.)

Shown in the early 1960s, this Ulrichsen boat, the *Carleton Island*, was donated to Association Island from the Frederick and Isabel Shick family boathouse on Carleton Island in the St. Lawrence River. Its arrival at the former dock at Brown Cottage on Hovey's Island is an extremely rare look at the large docking facility on the southeastern shore of Hovey's Island, now long gone. The gravel bar and Association Island are in the background. (Courtesy of Billings.)

When GE pulled out of Association Island, it coincided with the decline of many years of boatbuilding in Henderson Harbor. On August 15, 1966, this 28-foot caravel-planked Irwin fishing boat, built by Kent Irwin and David Cornell at Cornell's Marina for John Dunk, is being loaded into the water through a slip at the marina. Many Irwin lapstrake and plank boats were built in Henderson Harbor from the 1930s until 1976, when the last Irwin, a work-and-tow boat for Cornell's Marina, was crafted. These two boats and a third Irwin fishing boat from 1975 were still used in Henderson Harbor in 2012. (Courtesy of John Dunk.)

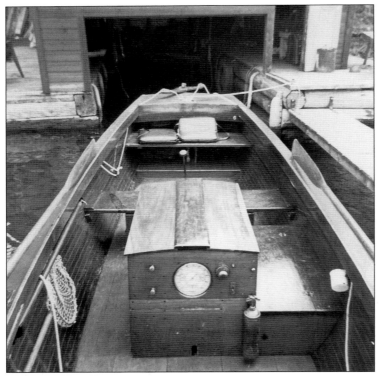

This is a classic Henderson Harbor guide boat from the 1930s. Equipped with an automobile engine beneath the compartment, these fishing boats also required oars for dependability. Henderson Harbor fishing guides Lyle and Robert McCrea, who both used the small cup on the right to scoop a drink of water out of the lake, owned this boat. It is docked at the McCrea boathouse at the Marquet Gardens cottage subdivision on Henderson Bay, formerly part of Rockledge farm. (Courtesy of McCrea.)

The Henderson Harbor guide boat was not very large but was ideal for navigating over the many shoals that produced black bass and perch. Early guided trips were limited to near-shore shoals at Hovey's, Association, Sixtown, Gull, and Bass Islands. Overnight trips were taken to Stony and Galloo Islands. On the Lyle and Robert McCrea guide boat from the 1930s, the shifting lever is aft of the engine compartment. Steering was accomplished by pulling on the ropes to turn the rudder. (Courtesy of McCrea.)

Seven

HENDERSON HARBOR

Prior to the NELC men arriving at Henderson Harbor in 1903, this is how the small fishing community appeared in this view looking south near Tyler's Inn along Harbor Road. Cottages, left, were small farmhouses. Boathouses, right, were built over the water along the edge of Harbor Road. In this c. 1900 photograph, the road is packed with dirt and gravel and lined with buggy tracks. The boat is a steamer, and the waterfront land, which is now along Reed Canal, right background, is a pasture.

The Capt. Elman and Cynthia Tyler farm along Harbor Road grew into the very popular Tyler's Inn and boat livery by 1900. In this photograph from about 1915 are, from left to right, Tyler's stone pagoda, the original boathouse converted to rooms, the skiff shed, and boathouse with a screened-in sitting room on the second floor. In the right background are the first of the cottages and boathouses that would appear on the north side of what later became Reed Canal.

Tyler's gradually expanded to include four large cottages, the pagoda, and boathouse. Pictured, from left to right, but partially hidden by trees, are the two-story inn, a cottage behind the pagoda, the original farmhouse, and the boathouse complex. In 1915, this would have been the view from across Henderson Harbor and the Colewood campground.

SUMMER HOME OF
MRS. B.R. STILLMAN
HENDERSON HARBOR N.Y.

North on Harbor Road from Tyler's Inn were a classic farmhouse cottage and boathouse, owned for many years by the Stillman and Junker families and later and presently by the family of H. Kaye Kerr, onetime consultant to Richard W. Billings on Association Island. This cottage burned in 1974. The classic boathouse, built of similar design as Tyler's boathouse, was still intact and being used in 2012. Note the gravel Harbor Road is lined with maple trees on the left and elm trees on the right. Tyler's Inn is in the background.

STATE ROAD AT WARNERS
HENDERSON HARBOR N.Y. NO. 5

In 1906, the NELC men purchased Warner's Island from George H. Warner, proprietor of Warner's Inn on the northeast side of Henderson Harbor. At about the same time, Warner built this Victorian cottage overlooking Henderson Bay and Association Island. The Warner farm was on the right, out of the picture. Next to this property were the waterfront lots that Warner sold to the Foster, Dulles, and Lansing families for their cottages.

This was the Warner farmhouse along Harbor Road as it appeared prior to construction of the family's waterfront Victorian cottage. Warner's Inn was very popular with Watertown and Syracuse, New York, residents who came to Henderson Harbor for trout fishing. The sunset view from the farmhouse porch looked over Warner's Island, later Association Island.

Also along Harbor Road near Warner's Inn was the Augustus and Clarissa Bassett cottage and boardinghouse. The Bassetts' son James and nephew LaMort handcrafted fine Henderson Harbor guide boats, some of which are pictured in this book. The view from the opposite side of the farmhouse on a bluff overlooking Henderson Bay was westerly toward Association Island.

LaMort W. Bassett, center, built this large brick cottage on Bassett's Bluff with a large porch overlooking Henderson Bay, left, and Association Island. The Bassett boatbuilding shop was across Harbor Road. Many Henderson Harbor families were proud owners of Bassett-built guide boats, and many of them were used at Association Island.

Between the Bassett cottage and Warner's Inn, Bernard and Gertrude Janssen of New York City, owners of the world-renowned Janssen Piano Company, built this cottage on the bluff overlooking Henderson Bay and Association Island. It was purchased about 1922 by John C. Marsellus and named Cedarbrook. Four generations of the Marsellus family spent summers at Cedarbrook.

This is what the heart of Henderson Harbor looked like in 1907 when the NELA campers first arrived at Association Island. On the left is Wilbur and MaryAnn Hammond's store. The photographer was standing in front of Snow's Hotel, which later became the original Harbor Inn. The portion of the Gill House under its sign was originally a boathouse that had been moved up from the waterfront for expansion.

The Hotel De Snow or Snow's Hotel was built about 1895 by Goodwin M. Snow on the waterfront where Harbor View Road meets Harbor Road in Henderson Harbor. On the left, double-ended rowing skiffs were pulled under the boathouse for protection. This photograph is labeled August 3, 1907. This location later became the main GE dock in Henderson Harbor.

HARBOR INN - HENDERSON HARBOR, N.Y.

In 1912, Goodwin M. Snow sold Snow's Hotel to Charles J. Purdy, a former lamp manufacturer who had sold his business to the NELA in 1909 and was an original investor in Association Island. Purdy renamed the hotel the Harbor Inn and, for the future growth of Association Island, invested $7,000 in the property, including the kitchen, dining room, and the docks. He also purchased a steamer to haul passengers and goods to the island. This is the view of the Harbor Inn and Marina complex from the water around 1915.

Nearly across Harbor Road from the Harbor Inn was the original post office. Goodwin M. Snow served as postmaster from 1924 until his death in 1930 at the age of 69. Because of his close and trusted relationship with so many GE executives, his obituary also appeared in Schenectady and New York City newspapers. Today, this building, pictured in 1937, is a private residence. (Courtesy of Lattimer.)

About the time the NELC men arrived in Henderson Harbor, the main business district along Harbor Road looked like this. Pictured, from left to right, along the dirt road looking north are Goodwin M. Snow's garage and store; Ontario Grocery, which later became Pilon's; the new

Henderson Harbor, N. Y.

Harbor Inn, Snow's Hotel; and the original Harbor Inn; and in the distance is the Frontier House, which was soon after renamed the Gill House.

This is the Henderson Harbor curve about 1910 in a view looking south toward the Gill House, left center. Known as the state road, Harbor Road was gravel and dirt and marked with buggy and tire tracks in 1910. Hugh and Minnie Gill's barn is in the center, and the cottage on the right is still standing today.

Prior to 1912, the Henderson Bay waterfront, located just north of the Harbor Inn and the Gill House at the curve, was owned by Hugh and Minnie Gill, proprietors of the Gill House. The renowned Gill apple orchard began on the right side of the road and stretched north nearly to Warner's Inn below Chestnut Ridge. Most of this land was sold to Watertown real estate developers in 1912 for a proposed cottage and boathouse community called Henderson Harbor Park.

The Harbor Inn became a popular place for visiting fishermen to pick up a guide and fish for trout in Lake Ontario. This group of fishermen is posing with several trout on the Harbor Inn dock about 1915. The trout fishery was depleted in Lake Ontario by the 1940s but was revived with a New York State trout-stocking program in the early 1970s.

In 1907, this would have been the view for Association Island campers approaching Henderson Harbor by boat. Snow's Hotel, which later became the original Harbor Inn, is the large building right center. The Gill House is left center and includes a small dock building on the waterfront.

In the years before motorboats, fishermen often spent several days on Stony or Galloo Islands because it took so long to get there by rowboats. In this photograph from the early 1930s on Stony Island, a large trout is part of the catch. (Courtesy of Joel Wescott.)

The Harbor Inn was for fishermen and visitors to Association Island, who could always find a cozy and warm fire, comfortable rooms, a bar, and good food. This photograph of the remodeled interior from about 1910 displays a large photograph of Association Island campers and a map of New York State on the wall next to the fireplace made of stones that are found in Henderson Harbor.

This view of the southeast end of Henderson Harbor shows the gravel and dirt state road, Harbor Road, with buggy and tire tracks. This photograph is dated 1909 and describes Tyler's Inn, seen on the left, in the heart of Henderson Harbor. The Stillman-Junker-Kerr cottage and boathouse are in the foreground.

Gardner's Grocery was a fixture on the waterfront in Henderson Harbor for many years. Originally Hammond's store and founded by Wilbur W. and MaryAnn Hammond, it was situated between the Gill House and Henchen Marina. Sisters Pearl and Hazel Hammond later operated it with a popular ice cream parlor. The building was demolished to make room for a sailboat and yacht basin, located on the site of the original Harbor Inn and the GE dock. (Courtesy of Church.)

The Gill House may be the most recognized landmark in Henderson Harbor. Originally the Frontier House when ship captain John S. Warner owned it, the inn was renamed Gill House when Hugh H. and Minnie C. Gill purchased it around the same time the NELC men first arrived at Henderson Harbor. Several additions turned the Gill House into the large and renowned inn and restaurant that it became by the 1950s. The Gill House regained its long and outstanding reputation for fine dining in 2012.

A boathouse from the shoreline was moved to the south side of the Gill House to create more rooms. A large porch was added to the northeast side of the inn overlooking a broad lawn leading down to Henderson Bay. This photograph is from about 1915, which was after GE had taken over at Association Island.

The original Gill House dock was on a point jutting into the water where Henderson Harbor joins Henderson Bay. In this photograph from the 1920s, it is a large T-shaped dock suitable for several large boats at a time. Three gentlemen are sitting at the end of the dock. The barn where Hugh H. Gill took his own life in 1917 because of poor health is at the far right.

The Gill's daughter Bessie Gill took over the popular inn after her father's death. When this photograph was taken in the summer of 1937, the Gill House had enjoyed a solid reputation for fish and chicken dinners and comfortable rooms for many years. Bessie Gill leased the facility as she got older and then sold it to Albert and Dorothy Miles, who continued its stellar reputation for many years. Financial pressure and legal wrangling closed the renowned restaurant just prior to its rebirth in 2012. (Courtesy of Lattimer.)

Known as the Elm Tree Inn when this photograph was taken in the 1930s, this renowned four-story Henderson Harbor hotel was on a hill above Aspinwall Shores on the southeast side of Henderson Harbor. From here, a long driveway led down to a complex of docks and boathouses on the water. This was the first Gill House, which was later razed; the Henderson Harbor Performing Arts Center is at this site today.

From the southeast, this view of Henderson Harbor in the 1940s shows the Elm Tree Inn, bottom center, and the tree-lined lane leading down to the water. Shown, from left to right, are Hovey's Island, Association Island, Davis Island, and Sixtown Island. Just above the Elm Tree Inn are the recently constructed Cornell's Marina and Reed Canal before it was lined with boathouses. (Courtesy of Church.)

Warner's Island had been a favorite fishing site for this man, Wilson administration secretary of state Robert M. Lansing, around 1900 when he and fishing guide Will Stevens would row from Lansing's cottage to the island for a daylong fishing trip. About the time it became Association Island, Lansing and a group of Watertown men organized a fishing camp, the Fortnightly Club, on Galloo Island, where this photograph was taken in the early 1920s. (Courtesy of JCHS.)

Located next to his in-laws' large Victorian cottage Underbluff along Harbor Road, Secretary Lansing's cottage, pictured, commanded a beautiful sunset view of Association Island. Association Island campers sent two pies across the bay to Lansing's cottage Linden Lodge in July 1916. He replied to the pastry chef at Camp Claverack by letter, saying, "They have been enjoyed by me and my guests extremely." The woman paddling is believed to be Eleanor Lansing Dulles in the 1920s. (Courtesy of David Joor.)

A Henderson Harbor landmark in 2012, Lake Lodge Hotel was established on a small bluff across Harbor Road from Pilon's Dock and Store in the 1930s. Long a favorite bar and restaurant for fishermen, it has been altered dramatically from its appearance in this photograph in 1937. (Courtesy of Lattimer.)

Facing west and on a bluff, Lake Lodge Hotel was renamed Westview Lodge by the date of this photograph in the mid-1950s. Still a favorite of Henderson Harbor fishermen, it was named the Bill Saiff Westview Lodge and Marina in 2012. (Courtesy of Church.)

The Lookout Lunch commanded the best all-around view of Association Island. Perched high atop Chestnut Ridge and facing northwest, the tower was built for an observation deck next to the public parking lot along New York State Route 3, which was constructed on the ridge above Henderson Harbor in 1933–1934. From here, visitors can see beyond Association Island to Canada.

Henderson Harbor residents all agree that winters in northern New York State are challenging. However, very few visitors to Association Island, seen at center, ever experienced them because the island was closed for winter. In this photograph on March 3, 1950, from the Chestnut Ridge parking lot next to Lookout Lunch, Henderson Bay is covered with ice. Early Henderson Harbor residents routinely drove horse-drawn sleighs, and later cars and trucks, across the ice to the islands. (Courtesy of Janine Smith.)

Snowshoe Bay, pictured at the bottom right, ends at the gravel bar between Snowshoe Point and Hovey's Island. The navigation canal known as the Cut, found at right center, was opened in September 1927 with GE and local residents splitting the $7,000 cost. By the time this photograph was taken, the GE golf course on the former Winnie and Martha Hovey farm, bottom right, had returned to farmland. Stony Island is at the top right, and the former Stony Point Rifle Range is at the top left. (Courtesy of Church.)

Reed Canal and most of its long boathouses were completed by 1950. Spoils from the canal were used to create extra land at the canal entrance, and this is where the Henderson Harbor Yacht Club (HHYC) was relocated, pictured at left center, in 1946 after moving out of the former Tyler's boathouse, seen at top left. The road on the right is the tree-lined lane that led to the Elm Tree Inn, the original Gill House. (Courtesy of Church.)

In this view of Reed Canal from the west, the HHYC is under construction on the point. The Phelps and Cornell Marina is on the left, and the tree-lined lane running from the waterfront up to the original Gill House, Elm Tree Inn, and later, O'Donnell's Hotel, is on the right. (Courtesy of Church.)

Four brothers from the well-known Wescott family of Henderson Harbor were deployed in World War II. On April 16, 1945, Pfc. Ray Wescott Jr., USMC, left, greets his brother, Seaman Albert Wescott, USCG, aboard ship in Mindanao, the Philippines. Their brothers Herbert and Joseph Wescott served in the US Merchant Marine and the US Navy. They were the sons of Ray and Eunice Wescott and part of the last family to live on Stony Island. After the war, Ray Wescott Jr. worked as a pilot on Association Island ferryboats.

The Herbert and Bertha Hess Wescott family was the last to live on and make their living on Stony Island. Their island farmhouse, pictured here, faced Stony Point and the mainland about eight miles from Association Island. After leaving the island in the 1930s, some of the Wescott boys worked as boatbuilders, along with their neighbor George Irwin, in Henderson. Other Wescott family members owned the farm that is Wescott Beach State Park and were related to local families with names such as Bovee and Hess, who also worked at Association Island.

Black bass and perch fishing have always attracted fishermen to Henderson Harbor and the shoals around Association Island. Expert fishing guides included Robert McCrea, left, and his father, Lyle, who ran his 23-foot fishing boat *El-To-Pay* for many years. Their first guide boat is seen in chapter 6. Robert's son David McCrea was still working as a Henderson Harbor fishing guide with his boat *El-To-Pay* in 2012. (Courtesy of McCrea.)

Occasionally, Association Island–based boaters needed a rescue from the lake. The Galloo Island Coast Guard Base was located on the southeastern shore of Galloo Island and was only a 20-minute boat ride from Association Island. Established in 1936, this base was closed in 1972 when operations were moved to Sackets Harbor. (Courtesy of CGH.)

The PK Clubhouse, a gentleman's fishing club also known as the Fortnightly Club, was at North Pond on the northwest side of Galloo Island. Made up of mostly businessmen from Watertown, New York, the most prominent member was US secretary of state Robert M. Lansing, shown on the right pitching a horseshoe in the 1920s. He kept his summer home in Henderson Harbor. In their boats from Henderson Harbor, the men had to navigate around Association Island to reach Galloo Island and their clubhouse. (Courtesy of JCHS.)

Originally part of Warner's farm on the northeast side of Henderson Harbor, these classic bay-front cottages were mostly built between 1910 and 1930. Given names such as Bluebird, Overstone, and Cedarbrook, these cottages and boathouses, with their foundations in the bay, faced the sunsets and Association Island. The Foster, Dulles, and Lansing cottages were just to the right of this picture. (Courtesy of Church.)

The Oliver J. McConnell boathouse, pictured here about 1920, faced the west toward Colewood campground in Henderson Harbor. McConnell was a Sandy Creek and Pierrepont Manor, New York, farmer who later made his fortune in mining and logging in Montana. His classic boathouse became the most popular marina and bait shop in Henderson Harbor when it was purchased in 1937 by Charles and Lottie Henchen and opened as Henchen Marina in 1938.

Henchen Fishing Camp and Marina was located along Harbor Road just south of the new Harbor Inn, shown at right, which was formerly Pilon's Dock and Ontario Grocery. The fishermen's cabins were built in the 1940s by local carpenters and fishing guides, including Ruddy Ditch. The marina remained in the Henchen family with Robert and Diane Henchen Gamble until 2005. In 2011, it was still the busiest marina in Henderson Harbor. (Courtesy of Church.)

George and Evelyn Henchen took over the family marina and bait shop in 1962. By this time, GE was gone from Association Island, but bass and perch fishing in eastern Lake Ontario was at its apex. With gas to pump, bait to sell, and fish to clean, the Henchens were some of the busiest merchants in Henderson Harbor from May through October. (Courtesy of Church.)

From this location at the GE dock in Henderson Harbor, Association Island visitors often checked the departure time of their boat for the island and then walked down Harbor Road, past the signs, to Henchen Marina to purchase bait that they would carry to Association Island. This scene is from 1956, with buses having just arrived with island visitors from the train station. (Courtesy of miSci.)

Henchen's Restaurant was built in 1954 across Harbor Road from the marina. George and Evelyn Henchen operated the restaurant for many years until it was sold to become a popular bar and restaurant, which is operating still today as Rydolph's Café and Lounge. (Courtesy of Henchen.)